Is there an english menu? *Sumimasen.* Excuse me. *Omizu onegaishimasu.* A glass of water please.

...nishimasu. Please bring me this. *Omakase shimasu.* Please bring me the chef's choice.

delicious. *Okanjō onegaishimasu.* Please bring the bill. *Kādo de ii desu ka?* May I pay with a credit card?

As always to my husband Frank,
my Mother who taught me to appreciate good food
and to our friends in Japan
with whom we have shared many wonderful meals.

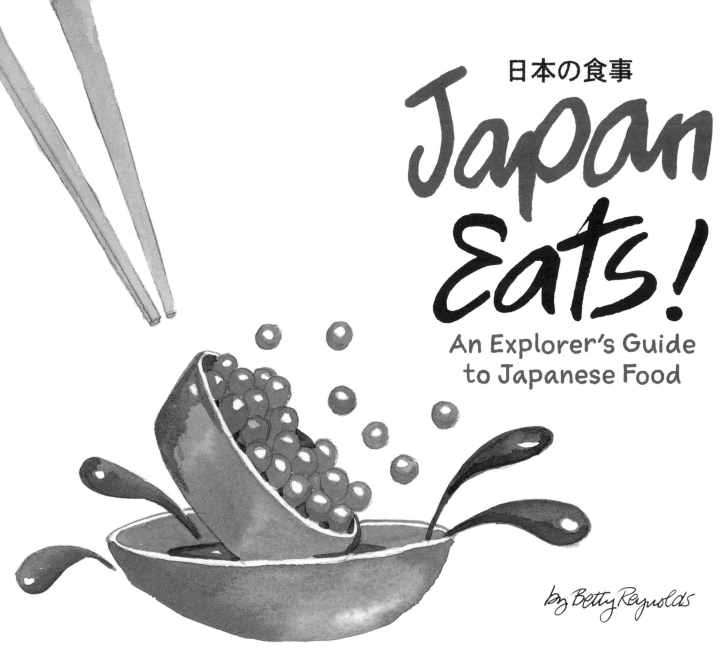

日本の食事

Japan Eats!

An Explorer's Guide to Japanese Food

by Betty Reynolds

TUTTLE Publishing

Tokyo | Rutland, Vermont | Singapore

Contents
Please enjoy!

いただきます
"Itedakimasu!"
"I receive/accept this with thanks"

In Japan, even the most humble meal begins with a slight bow and the expression "Itedakimasu". To help you remember this phrase, think of this English mnemonic: "Eat a duck I must."

おしぼり
Oshibori
Neatly re-fold after using with the soiled bits facing inward

ちゃわん
Chawan
rice bowl
Soy sauce and food should not be placed on rice

やきものざら
yakimono
dish for grilled fish

ゆのみぢゃわん
yunomi-jawan
cup for green tea

しるわん
Shiru-wan
soup bowl
Squeeze here to break the seal if the lid is stuck

place lid to the right with inside facing up

Sometimes there is a beautiful design inside.

← My friends make a origami chopstick rest out of the paper case

おはし
Ohashi chopsticks should always point to the left

Irasshaimase!
welcome!

Eating in Japan is an absolute delight and one of the pleasures of living or traveling there, but to the non-Japanese eating out can be a confusing experience. At least it was for me when my husband and I moved to Tokyo in 1994. At first we were inhibited by the language barrier, indecipherable signs and menus, plus our general lack of Japanese culture. But soon we realized that our forays out were always an adventure. We received some food we didn't know we ordered and ate some things

7:30pm   7:45   8:00

Remember-you may not be as limber as your Japanese hosts. Stretch your legs every we never thought we would eat–but usually even the consequences of our mistakes were delicious.

In time, as we made Japanese friends we were introduced to unique experiences and incredibly delicious food. This sketchbook is a reflection of those many meals shared. I hope it will help people better appreciate Japanese cuisine, whether they are dining in Tokyo's Ginza or a local Japanese restaurant anywhere in the world.

Goran kudasai! Please take a look

8:15   8:30   8:45

fifteen minutes and don't be surprised if you have to be pried up off the floor!

POISSON

六三四

そば

しゃぶ
しゃぶ

天丼

おでん

酒館

The noren advertises the restaurants name or type of Cuisine

高木　天

のれん **Noren:** A curtain hanging outside

ふぐ
Fugu
this hanging fish means poisonous pufferfish are served inside

Signs of importance

Choosing a restaurant when you can't read kanji, hiragana and katakana can be a bit tricky. Here are some clues to help you find your way.

Beware of shops with dusty plastic food!

サンプル
Sanpuru
plastic food samples outside represent the cusine inside. This is extremely helpful for beginners.

6

ぷら

means the restaurant is open for business

あかちょうちん
Aka chōchin
hanging lanterns
mean inexpensive
eating and
drinking
places

おでん

いらっしゃいませ
"Irasshaimase!"
"Welcome!"

If people hoot
and holler when
you enter
it means they are
glad to see you.

If however, they
cross their arms
they mean go away
please return
another time.

じゅんびちゅう
junbi chū
(preparation
time)
please come
back later

Close

準備中

7

メニュー
menyū
menus with colored photos are a godsend. You can thank your lucky stars when you receive one ↓

たたみ
tatami ↑
straw mat flooring

おかんじょう
okanjō
Those little pieces of paper (that you can't read) are bills.

Normally you pay on your way out.

Many restaurants have an inner floor called tatami. The Japanese are fastidious about their inner space. It is important to step out of your shoes and onto the tatami without dirtying your socks.

Some restaurants require you to remove your shoes, and change into slippers in the entry way. Remove your slippers at the entrance of the tatami.

くつ
kutsu
shoes
Always take off your shoes or slippers before stepping on tatami. Place them neatly please. Tuck in your shoelaces.

スリッパ
surippa
slippers
step into slippers provided for trips to the toilet.

トイレのスリッパ
toire-no surippa
toilet slippers
Once inside the toilet step into the plastic toilet slippers. Don't forget to remove them when you leave.

"Disorganized shoes are a sign of disorderly thinking" old Buddhist proverb.

Help me please! Where oh where is the toilet?

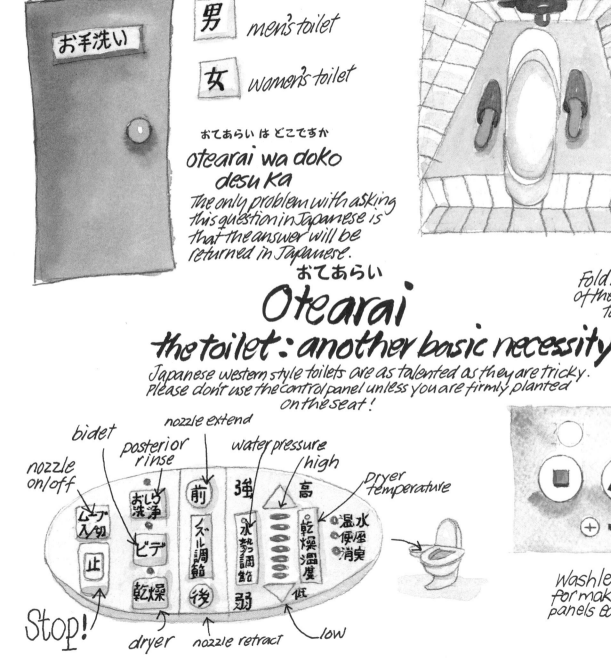

男　men's toilet

女　women's toilet

おてあらい は どこですか

otearai wa doko desu ka

The only problem with asking this question in Japanese is that the answer will be returned in Japanese.

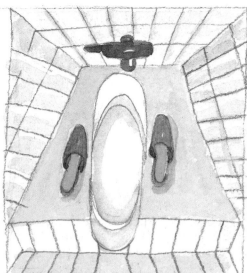

At the risk of being too familiar I'd like to explain how to use the Asian toilet. Face inward, straddle the toilet and squat as low as you can. Go slowly to avoid splashing shoes.

おてあらい

Otearai
the toilet: another basic necessity

Japanese western style toilets are as talented as they are tricky. Please don't use the control panel unless you are firmly planted on the seat!

Fold in the edges of the toilet paper to show respect for the next person!

nozzle on/off

bidet

posterior rinse

nozzle extend

water pressure high

Dryer temperature

ムーブ 入切

おしり 洗浄

ビデ

乾燥

前

ノズル調節

後

強

水勢調節

弱

高

乾燥温度

低

温水便座消臭

Stop!

dryer

nozzle retract

low

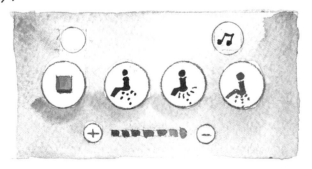

Washlet designers: Thank you for making the newer control panels easier to understand.

You can always point to another diner's meal when you can't read the menu

Yes
↑ the correct way to hold ohashi

Required Finger skills

Most Japanese meals are eaten with wooden sticks called Ohashi. They require a little skill and patience. **gambatte!** (Do your best)

← NO! It is considered impolite to spear your food

おしぼり
Oshibori
A moist hand towel will be brought to your table

おはし
Ohashi
chopsticks →

Hey! Where is my soup spoon?

Lift your bowl to your chest. Use the ohashi to eat the morsels, then sip the broth directly from the bowl.

Don't fret if you only receive one big stick— pry them apart at the narrow end.

Waribashi
Half-split chopsticks

(Disposable)

You mustn't dig into a central serving dish with your used chopsticks. If there are no serving chopsticks—turn your own and use the thicker ends. (which should be unsoiled if you were paying attention.)

Hold your cup in both hands. The left hand should support the cup

Use your chopsticks to transport the rice to your mouth.

Hold your rice bowl at a comfortable level

When drinking soup hold the bowl to your mouth using both hands.

Re-usable collapsible chopsticks come with their own travel case

Don't worry about making a mistake. We foreigners are forgiven almost anything. Just enjoy!

Sashimi さしみ

literally means "fresh slice" – but a more common definition is raw seafood

おつくり
otsukuri
← creative presentation of a course of sashimi

しょうゆ
shōyu
soy sauce

What is considered bait in one country is a gourmet meal in another. Surrounded by ocean, Japanese people will put absolutely anything from the sea into their mouths.
And if fresh is good, then alive is even better!

Sushi すし
vinegared rice

すしおけ
Sushi oke
Container
for serving
Sushi

Sushi or nigirizushi, as it is known here in Tokyo, is an oblong of vinegared rice with a smear of wasabi and is covered with a topping of raw or cooked seafood or some other ingredient. For the novice, sushi is a safer order since it never arrives gasping at the table.

おおとろ
Ō-Toro
tuna belly

まぐろ
Maguro
tuna

ひらめ
Hirame
halibut

はまち
Hamachi
yellowtail

すずき
Suzuki
sea bass

さけ
Sake
salmon

えび
Ebi
prawn

にぎりずし
Nigirizushi
Tokyo sushi

Sushi can be ordered as a fixed-price set but it is much more fun to sit at the counter and order directly from the chef.

Devotees usually start with an order of sashimi. With sushi they begin with the more subtle flavors of lighter, white fish, moving onto the fattier, stronger tastes. The meal often ends with tamago-yaki (sweet omelette.)

いたまえさん
Itamae san
chef

げた
geta
some sushi chefs wear high platform shoes to keep their feet dry

かずのこ
Kazunoko
herring roe

かつお
Katsuo
bonito

たい
Tai
sea bream

14

あまえび
Ama-ebi
sweet prawn

しめさば
Shime saba
mackerel

たこ
Tako
octopus

いか
Ika
squid

いくら
Ikura
salmon roe

とびこ
Tobiko
flying fish roe

うに
Uni
sea urchin roe

がり
Gari
pickled ginger

ほたてがい
Hotategai
scallop

とりがい
Torigai
cockle

あじ
Aji
horse mackerel

Agari
green tea
あがり

うなぎ
Unagi
freshwater eel

あなご
Anago
sea eel

みるがい
Mirugai
horse clam

あかがい
Akagai
ark shell

あわび
Awabi
abalone

こはだ
Kohada
gizzard shad

たまごやき
Tamago-yaki
omelette

しょうゆ
shōyu
soy sauce

Please use sparingly.
It is considered wasteful
to fill your bowl
too full.

It could also be considered dangerous when you are not skillful with chopsticks. You could end up with stains on your and your neighbor's clothing!

Sushi tips
I've learned the hard way

It is perfectly acceptable —
and maybe even advisable
to use your fingers.

Dip the
topping
into the
soy sauce

Or end up
with rice
everywhere.

わさび
Wasabi
spicy
Japanese
horseradish

ひねしょうが
hine-shōga
grated ginger

がり
gari
vinegared
ginger is
eaten between
bites to cleanse
the palette

べにたで
beni tade

flowers of
the shiso plant

あぶない
abunai!
danger!
A little bit goes
a long, long way

There are stories circulating
about unsuspecting Westerners
who have popped the whole wad of
wasabi into their mouths and then
imploded.

ほしそ
ho shiso →
scrape off
downwards and
add to soy sauce

だいこん
daikon →
radish aids the
digestion

Don't be dainty
and try to bite
the sushi in half.

eat

きく
kiku
chrysanthemum

しそ
shiso
leaf of the
beefsteak
plant

don't eat →

さいくざさ
saikuzasa
bamboo grass-used
for decoration only!

17

Haven't I seen you someplace before?

Sometimes a piece of sushi has been around the block a couple of times. Check to see if the rice is still moist.

Sit near a sushi chef so that you can choose his freshly-made pieces. If you don't see what you want-ask for it.

You won't receive a bill. Simply wind your way to the cash register (usually near the front door.) You will be charged by the number of your discarded plates.

Plates are color-coded according to the price of the sushi

Help yourself to hot water and teabags

かいてんずし

What goes around—comes around

Kaiten-zushi

Conveyor belt sushi

A fun and less expensive way to eat sushi is to sit at a counter and make your selections from a revolving conveyor belt.

うめしそまき
ume-shiso maki
pickled plum and shiso leaf

なっとうまき
natto-maki
fermented soybean

ねぎとろまき
negi-toro-maki
long onion and raw tuna

サーモンスキンロール
sāmon-sukin-rōru
Salmon skin roll

A temaki is rolled by hand

てまきずし
Temaki-zushi
cone shaped makizushi

いなりずし
Inari-zushi
sushi rice in deep-fried tofu pouches

ふとまき
Futo-maki
Large rolls stuffed with pickled ginger, spinach, gourd

Sushi rice rolled in a sheet of nori (dried seaweed) and stuffed with veggies or raw fish with a dab of wasabi

まきずし

Makizushi

ちらしずし

Chirashizushi

and cucumber.

sashimi, vegetables, prawns, sweet omelette, fish eggs and other ingredients scattered on top of sushi rice.

makizushi is rolled in a bamboo mat called a makisu

21

たぬき

Tanuki
noodles in hot broth with fried tempura batter

きつね

Kitsune
noodles and broth with fried tofu and spring onion

つきみ

Tsukimi
noodles and broth with a raw egg

かもなんばん

Kamo-namban
noodles and broth with pieces of duck

Slurp! Slurp!

You're supposed to slurp to cool down the hot soup.

Slurp!

Forget everything
your Mother ever taught you about eating soup! The Japanese way is much more fun.

← You can pick up the bowl and drain the soup.

← You're allowed to stand up and eat at the table.

Why isn't anyone waiting on me?

Some noodle shops have a machine where you make your selection and buy a ticket. Present your ticket at the counter.

なべやきうどん

Nabeyaki-udon
Udon noodles and other ingredients cooked in an earthenware pot

22

そば と うどん

Soba & Udon
noodle dishes

Most Soba-ya serve soba and udon noodles. Specify your choice.

そば
Soba buck wheat & flour noodles

ちゃそば
cha-soba buckwheat, flour & tea noodles

Udon wheat flour noodles
うどん

てんぷらそば
Tempura soba noodles in hot broth with prawns fried in Tempura batter

← Often the tables & stools are so tiny that Westerners have trouble sitting side by side

やくみ
Yakumi condiments used to enhance the taste

わさび
Wasabi

negi ねぎ

しちみ
shichimi seven tastes spice

23

Cold noodles are very popular in summer.

Zaru-soba
ざるそば
Cold soba topped
with dried
seaweed
called nori

tokkuri
とっくり
container for sauce

taré
たれ
soy-based dipping sauce

choko
ちょこ
dipping cup

Sōmen
そうめん
Chilled wheat-based
noodles are served
on ice

yutō
ゆとう
square
lacquered
container

soba yu
そばゆ
pour the
hot broth the
noodles were cooked in
into your left-over
taré and drink like a
soup.

cha-soba
ちゃそば
flavored with
green tea

mori-soba
もりそば
Cold soba served
on a bamboo rack
in a lacquer box

みそラーメン
miso-rāmen
pork and vegetables in a miso-flavored broth

れいめん
rei-men
cold noodles with corn, cucumber, tomato, chicken and jellyfish

とんこつラーメン
tonkotsu-rāmen
pork and vegetables in pork and salt-flavored broth

ねぎラーメン
negi-rāmen
minced meat and long onion in a spicy broth

ラーメン　らーめん
Rāmen
chinese noodles

カレーラーメン
karē-rāmen
curry-flavored broth

チャーシューメン
chāshū-men
grilled pork, bamboo shoots, spring onions and nori or spinach in a soy-flavored broth

At last!
A soup spoon

ギョーザ
gyoza
fried dumplings

シューマイ
shūmai
steamed dumplings

Hot and delicious, rāmen is taken very seriously here. Everyone has their favorite soup and is willing to stand in line for it. Rāmen noodles are made of wheat flour, egg and salt. The noodles are boiled and served in a pork or chicken-based stock.

25

とんかつ

Tonkatsu
Fried breaded pork cutlet

ミートコロッケ

Mito-Korokke
Minced meat, onion and mashed potato croquette

Karé-raish
CURRY RICE

Popular with locals and tourists alike, curry rice has emerged as one of the top favorite cuisines in Japan.

You can also find curry in sandwiches and noodle soups.

オムライス

Omu-raisu
Ketchup-flavored rice pilaf wrapped in an omlette

ハヤシライス

Hayashi-raisu
Japanese beef hash served with rice

Closed during the day

open for business

おでんやたい
oden yatai
Oden stalls open in the evening. Their light's soft glow looks warm and inviting.

おでん
Oden
and other movable feasts

Oden, much more tasty than it looks, consists of healthy ingredients simmered in a fish broth. Select the pieces you want and dip into spicy mustard.

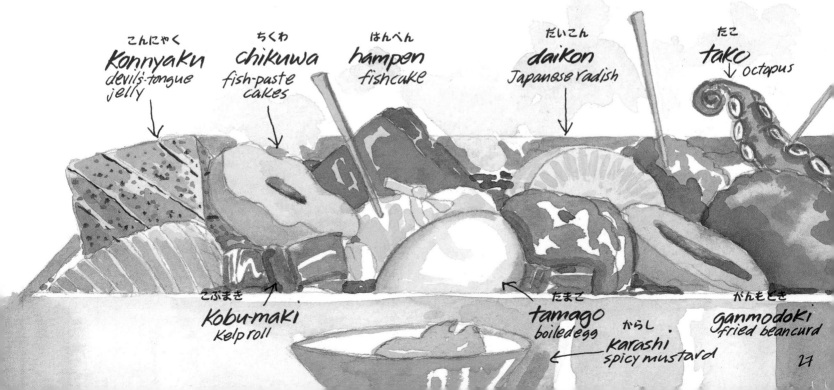

こんにゃく
Konnyaku devil's-tongue jelly

ちくわ
chikuwa fish-paste cakes

はんぺん
hampen fishcake

だいこん
daikon Japanese radish

たこ
tako octopus

こぶまき
Kobu-maki Kelp roll

たまご
tamago boiled egg

からし
Karashi spicy mustard

がんもどき
ganmodoki fried beancurd

てんぷらていしょく

tempura teishoku
A set meal consisting of assorted pieces of tempura, rice, pickles and miso soup

てんどん

どんぶり
domburi
a porcelain bowl for rice dishes

ten-don
tempura and rice with a soy based sauce

An embarassing true story - when I first arrived in Tokyo I confused the dipping sauce for miso soup and promptly drained it. I certainly gave the staff a good giggle.

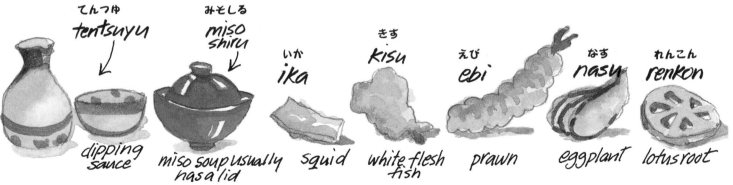

てんつゆ
tentsuyu
↓
dipping sauce

みそしる
miso shiru
↓
miso soup usually has a lid

いか
ika
squid

きす
kisu
white flesh fish

えび
ebi
prawn

なす
nasu
eggplant

れんこん
renkon
lotus root

Tempura

てんぷら

Seafood and vegetables, coated
in a light batter and deep-fried until crisp

We filled up on tempura in those early days, since that was some-
thing we recognized and could pronounce.
   In time we were taken to restaurants where we learned the
joy of sitting at a counter, and having hot, crispy morsels
delivered piece by delicious piece.

Add the daikon
(grated radish) to
the dipping sauce
or lightly dip
the tempura
in salt.

さつまいも	しいたけ	かぼちゃ	たまねぎ	かきあげ	ししとう	しそ	アスパラガス
Satsuma-imo	shiitake	Kabocha	tamanegi	Kakiage	shishitō	shiso	asuparagasu
sweet potato	mushroom	pumpkin	onion	lacy pancake	small sweet pepper	beefsteak plant	asparagus

Oh no! Do I have to cook that myself?
Being handed a plate of unfamiliar raw ingredients can be intimidating but the staff will be infinitely kind. Act clueless - and they will cook it for you.

すきやき
SUKiYAKi

First, melt the suet and grease the pot.

Saute the meat slightly.

Add the stock.

Add the other ingredients a few at a time, simmer until cooked.

Dip each ingredient into the beaten raw egg.

Raw egg is said to enhance the flavor of sukiyaki.

(Egg shells are free of disease here in Japan)

Do I really have to eat a raw egg?

ほりごたつ
horigotatsu (foot well)
You will probably sit Japanese-style at a low table. Some tables have a hidden well when you can place your legs.

わりした
warishita
Sukiyaki stock consisting of mirin (cooking saké), soy sauce and sugar

なべ
nabe
POT

ねぎ
negi
long onion

しゅんぎく
shungiku
edible chrysanthemum leaves

しいたけ
shiitake
mushroom

とうふ
tōfu
soybean curd

しらたき
shirataki
noodles made from konnyaku (a starch made from the devil's-tongue plant)

しもふりにく
shimofuri-niku
thinly sliced marbled beef

31

ごまだれ **gomadaré**
sauce made from sesame seeds, miso paste and soy sauce

ぽんず **ponzu**
vinegary sauce made from soy sauce and lemon

うすぎりにく **usugiri niku** thinly sliced beef or pork

しいたけ **shiitake** mushroom

やきどうふ **yakidōfu** grilled tofu

はくさい **hakusai** chinese cabbage

shirataki konnyaku noodles
しらたき

ねぎ **negi** long onion

えのき **enoki** mushroom

shimeji mushroom
しめじ

だし **dashi**
stock made from bonito flakes and kelp

しゃぶしゃぶ

Shabu-shabu

Periodically skim off the foam with the slotted spoon

Shabu-shabu is another popular (but expensive) meat dish. Swish the beef into the boiling broth and say "Shabu-shabu". The meat is ready to eat. Dip into one of the sauces. Slowly add the other ingredients, saving the noodles for last.

"No-pan shabu-shabu" (no panties) publicized by the financial scandal of 1998 is <u>much</u> more <u>expensive</u>.

1. Beat the egg. Combine with flour and water to make the batter.

2. Add your chosen ingredients:

キャベツ **kyabetsu** shredded cabbage

えび **ebi** prawn

いか **ika** squid

ぶた **buta** pork

agedama あげだま small chunks of fried tempura batter

3. Pour the mixture on the hotplate. Cook on both sides.

These create-your-own pancakes are cooked on a table with a built-in griddle. They are hearty and fun to eat—but don't expect blueberries and butter milk

おこのみやき
Okonomiyaki

"As-you-like-it" pancake

てっぱん **teppan** hot plate

4. Add the following toppings:

べにしょうが **beni shoga** vinegared ginger

あおのり **aonori** seaweed flakes

かつおぶし **katsuo-bushi** bonito flakes

マヨネーズ **mayonēzu** mayonnaise

おこのみやきソース **okonomiyaki sōsu** sauce made from ketchup, soy and Worcestershire

33

oroshi おろし
grated daikon with quail egg

Food on sticks

Yakitori
やきとり

Yakitori consists of 4 or 5 pieces of meat, skewered on a bamboo stick, dipped in sauce and grilled over a charcoal fire. Almost every part of the chicken is used in a set course - so if you're not fond of innards it is better to order ala carte.

さんしょう
sanshō herb spice

しちみ
shichimi seven-taste spice

やきとり・
Yakitori chicken thigh

つくね
tsukuné minced chicken

きも
Kimo liver

とりかわ
tori-Kawa chicken skin

かっぱなんこつ
Kappa nan Kotsu cartilage

すなぎも
sunagimo giblets

ぎんなん
ginnan gingko nut

ししとう
shishitō green, sweet (not hot) peppers

shiitake mushroom
しいたけ

34

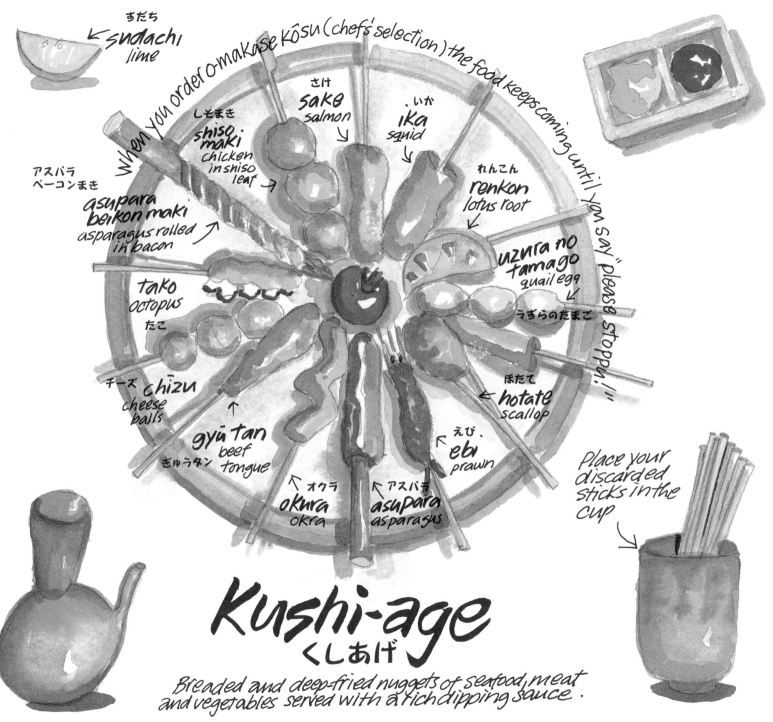

すだち
← **sudachi**
lime

When you order o-makase kōsu (chef's selection) the food keeps coming until you say "please stoppu!!"

しそまき
shiso maki
chicken in shiso leaf →

さけ
sake
salmon →

いか
ika
squid →

アスパラ
ベーコンまき
asupara beikon maki
asparagus rolled in bacon →

れんこん
renkon
lotus root

tako
octopus
たこ

uzura no tamago
quail egg
うずらのたまご

チーズ **chīzu**
cheese balls

ほたて
← **hotate**
scallop

↑ **gyū tan**
beef tongue
ぎゅうタン

えび
ebi
prawn

オクラ
okura
okra

アスパラ
asupara
asparagus

Kushi-age
くしあげ

Breaded and deep-fried nuggets of seafood, meat and vegetables served with a rich dipping sauce.

Place your discarded sticks in the cup →

The choice of Sumō wrestlers
Nabé なべ
Hotpot

Nothing satisfies a big appetite like a big hearty meal. Nabémono is the staple diet of sumōtori. Good for the body—and good for the soul! Especially in winter.

What do Sumó wrestlers eat? Anything they want!

ちゃんこなべ

Chanko-nabé

There are endless varieties of chanko nabé but the most popular version contains chicken, mushrooms, tofu, potatoes and vegetables simmered in a full-flavored stock.

よせなべ

Yosé-nabé

Contains an assortment of seafood: fish, prawns and clams as well as vegetables.

かきなべ

Kaki-nabé

Fresh oysters and miso paste makes this dish different than the others.

miso

あんこうなべ

Anko-nabé

Angler fish from the sea are added to the normal ingredients.

37

なまがき
Nama gaki
raw oysters

やきざかな
Yakizakana
broiled or grilled fish

かいそうサラダ
Kaisou sarada
seaweed salad

てばさき
Tebasaki
grilled chicken wings

でんがく
Dengaku
Konnyaku paste or tofu broiled with miso

びんビール
bin bīru

なまビール
Nama bīru
draft beer

しろワイン
Shiro wain

あかワイン
Aka wain

チューハイ
chū hai
shōchū and juice

かんざけ
Kanzaké
warm saké (rice wine)

ひやざけ
Hiya zaké
saké at room temperature.

bottled beer

SAPPORO

white wine

red wine

(Don't eat the pods)

O-toushi

ひややっこ

An appetizer of vegetables or raw fish will be brought to your table.

えだまめ

Edamame
Boiled beans in salted pods

Hiya-yakko
Chilled tofu

Izakaya いざかや

An Izakaya is a friendly place to eat and drink. Some are traditional while others are very hip. Sharing food and swapping stories in an Izakaya is my favorite way to unwind. After a few beers you are likely to meet everyone sitting close by.

やきにく

なすのでんがく

Yaki niku
pork marinated in soy sauce, ginger, garlic and sugar

Nasu-no-dengaku
Eggplant with miso sauce

The staff will always shout "Welcome" when you enter and "Thanks" when you leave. I don't know about you-but even my Mother doesn't seem this happy to see me!

Konbini コンビニ

Convenience Store

Japan has many of these stores selling delicious healthy meals, baked goods, beverages and sweets. The variety is endless and wonderfully Japanese. Seasonal and limited-editions fly off the shelves. Choose a meal to take back to your room, or micro-wave it and eat right there.

ビール
もも

Seasonal fruit-flavored beer and sweets →

chocolate cream in soft bread ↓

おむすび
Omubushi

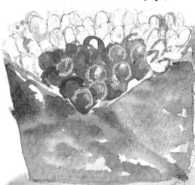

Rice balls filled with all manner of ingredients

おべんとう
O-Bento

Complete cooked meal offering fish, or meat, vegetables and rice

Yakisoba pan
やきそばパン

Fried-noodle sandwich

Kara-Age
からあげ

Crispy-fried chicken

Purin
プリン

プリン

Creamy pudding

The konbini offers other conveniences too - ATM's for cash withdrawal, or currency exchange, copy and ticket machines, shipping and bike rentals. They also offer personal items like shampoo, socks and underwear. One of my Japanese friends told me her family uses their local konbini as their refrigerator.

Chukka-man
ちゅうかまん

Chinese steamed bun filled with curry

Oden
おでん

Select your favorites from a warm broth and spice with mustard

Oyakko Don
おやこどん

Chicken and egg over rice

41

Mind you don't get run over by one of the many conveyances

Breakfast at Tsukiji

TSUKIJI OUTER MARKET

The wholesale market and tuna auction moved to Toyosu, but Tsukiji outer market still has lots to offer. There are hundreds of popular foodstalls, shops & restaurants. Get there early before the tours start at 10:00 am.

たまごやき

Tamago-yaki

もろこしあげ

Morokoshi-age

Sweet omelette

Croquette made with fish paste and sweet corn

Please don't eat while walking. Eat in designated areas instead.

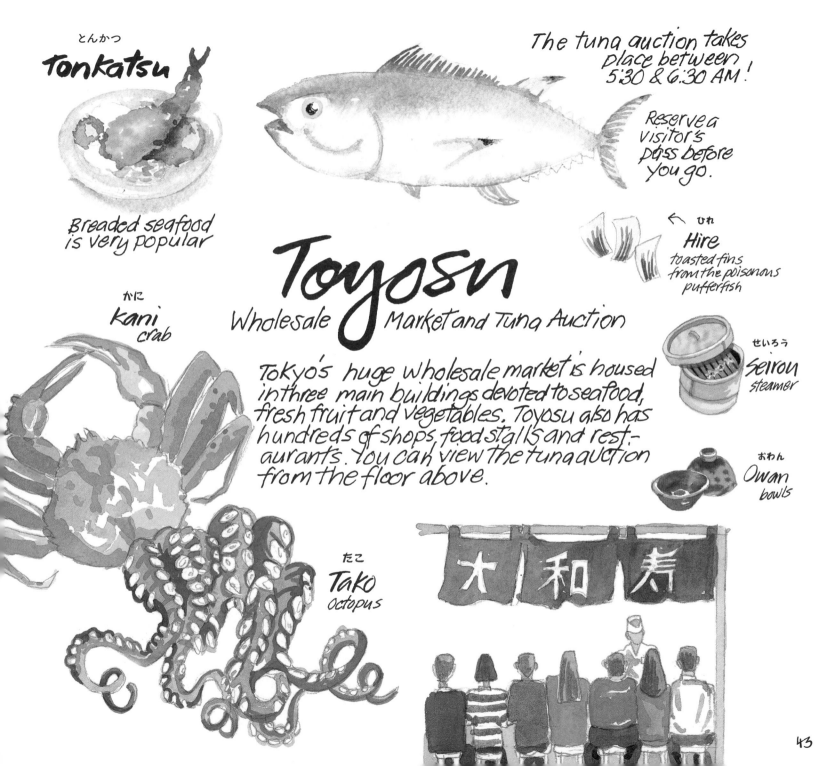

Tonkatsu
とんかつ

Breaded seafood is very popular

The tuna auction takes place between 5:30 & 6:30 AM!

Reserve a visitor's pass before you go.

← ひれ **Hire**
toasted fins from the poisonous pufferfish

かに **Kani**
crab

Toyosu
Wholesale Market and Tuna Auction

Tokyo's huge wholesale market is housed in three main buildings devoted to seafood, fresh fruit and vegetables. Toyosu also has hundreds of shops, food stalls and restaurants. You can view the tuna auction from the floor above.

せいろう **Seirou**
steamer

おわん **Owan**
bowls

たこ **Tako**
octopus

大和寿

43

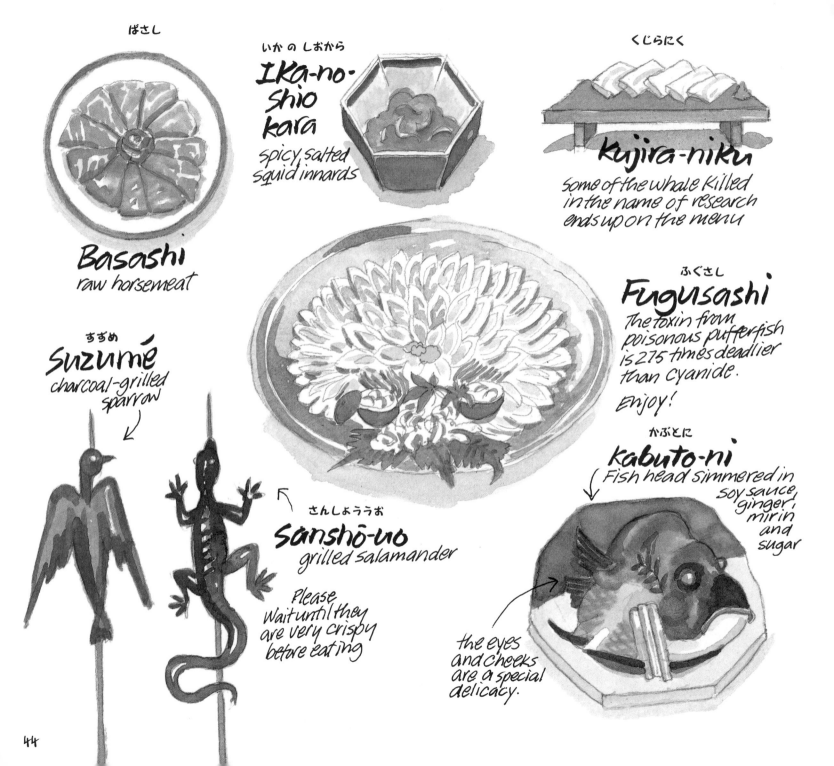

ばさし

Basashi
raw horsemeat

いか の しおから

IKa-no-Shio kara
spicy, salted squid innards

くじらにく

Kujira-niku
some of the whale Killed
in the name of research
ends up on the menu

ふぐさし

Fugusashi
The toxin from
poisonous pufferfish
is 275 times deadlier
than Cyanide.

Enjoy!

すずめ

Suzumé
charcoal-grilled
sparrow

さんしょううお

Sanshō-uo
grilled salamander

Please
Wait until they
are very crispy
before eating

かぶとに

Kabuto-ni
Fish head simmered in
soy sauce,
ginger,
mirin
and
sugar

the eyes
and cheeks
are a special
delicacy.

44

Hellooo. Is my dinner still breathing?

すがたづくり
Sugata-zukuri
Sashimi so fresh it is still moving

どじょうなべ
Dojō-nabé
live loach swimming in a pot (until cooked)

いけづくり
Ikezukuri
live seafood and other treats _not_ for the faint-hearted

しらうお の おどりぐい
Shirauo-no-odorigui
tiny live fish swimming in a liquid are meant to be swallowed whole. they quiver the whole way down.

えびおどり
Ebi odori
rip the heads off of live prawns and have them dance in your mouth

Iidako いいだこ
Some restaurants specialize in live seafood. Live baby octopus is difficult to keep in your mouth.

45

だるまべんとう

Daruma bentō
Seasoned meat and vegetables served in a plastic Daruma doll

ぜんこうじべんとう

Zenkōji bentō
Seasonal foods from Nagano

いかめし

Ika·meshi
Simmered squid stuffed with rice.

しゃないはんばいいん

shanai-hambai-in
The employees with food carts usually bow when they exit your train car.

さけ

Saké
rice wine

One cup

たのしみ

たのしみ

スナック

Sunakku
snacks of dried squid and octopus

えき

eki
train station

しんかんせん

Shinkansen
Bullet train

うなぎめし

Unagi-meshi
Grilled eel on rice

One of the experiences of traveling in Japan is enjoying the eki-ben (boxed lunch.) Many varieties are sold on the train and in train stations.
Wash them down with rice wine, beer or green tea.

えきべん
Eki-ben
Box lunches and other train treats

ミックスサンドイッチ

Mikkusu-sando itchi
An assortment of sandwiches- usually tuna, egg-salad and ham and cheese.

eye-sue-koo-reem-moo

アイスクリーム
aisu kurimu
Ice cream is sold in tiny containers

とうげのかまめし
Tōge-no-kamameshi
Rice, chicken, mushrooms, burdock root, bamboo shoot, veggies and boiled egg served in an earthenware container.

きっぷ
← **Kippu**

A doit　¥780

Misspelling on a local train ticket in Kyushu

Irori: Some Inns have irori (open hearths) where your fish and meat are grilled.

しゅんのたべもの

Shun-no-tabemono
Food that evokes the feeling of the season.

Dining and staying over in a traditional Japanese Inn is one of the great pleasures in life but for the non-Japanese it can be a cultural minefield. Just knowing what to do with your footwear requires an education.

Ryokan Ryòri

Japanese Inn Cuisine

おしぼり
oshibori
Moist hand towel

おかし
Okashi
Japanese sweet

にほんちゃ
Nihon-cha
Japanese tea

なかいさん
Nakai-san
Your gracious hostess and server will welcome you into your room with tea and a sweet.

Check-in time 3:00 pm

Check-out time 11:00am

Leave your shoes in the entrance way and slip into the slippers provided without dirtying your socks. Leave your shoes below the step.

Your incredibly tiny hostess will insist on carrying your bags to your room.

Leave your slippers in the entry of your room facing outwards.

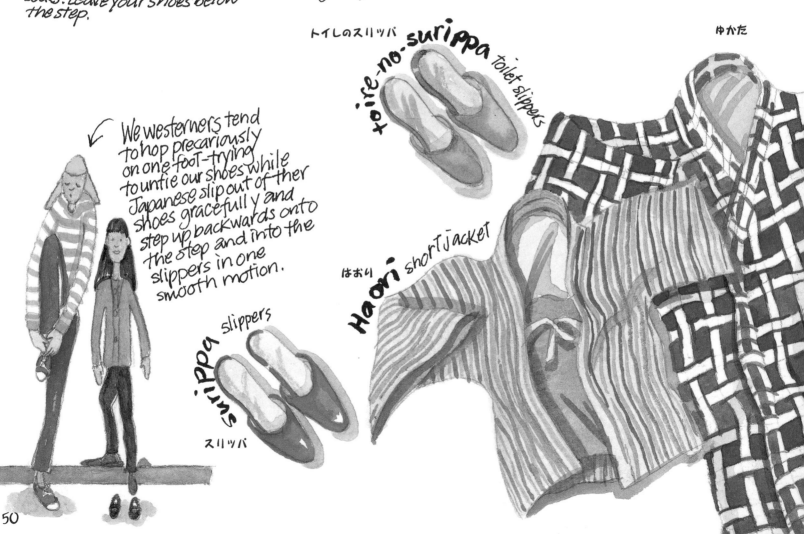

We westerners tend to hop precariously on one foot-trying to untie our shoes while Japanese slip out of ther shoes gracefully and step up backwards onto the step and into the slippers in one smooth motion.

トイレのスリッパ
toire-no-surippa toilet slippers

ゆかた

Haori short jacket
はおり

surippa slippers
スリッパ

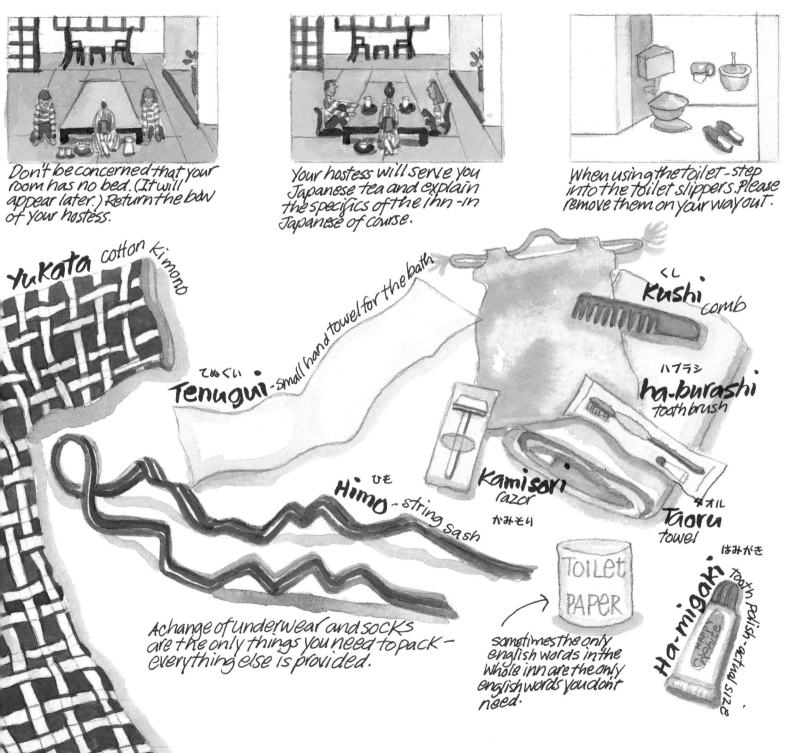

Don't be concerned that your room has no bed. (It will appear later.) Return the bow of your hostess.

Your hostess will serve you Japanese tea and explain the specifics of the inn – in Japanese of course.

When using the toilet – step into the toilet slippers. Please remove them on your way out.

Yukata cotton Kimono

Tenugui てぬぐい – small hand towel for the bath

Himo ひも – string sash

Kamisori razor かみそり

Kushi くし comb

ha-burashi ハブラシ tooth brush

Taoru タオル towel

Ha-migaki はみがき tooth polish – actual size

A change of underwear and socks are the only things you need to pack – everything else is provided.

TOILET PAPER

sometimes the only english words in the whole inn are the only english words you don't need.

51

Take your yukata, haori, towel and amenity kit with you to the ofuro (bath.) Once again, leave your slippers in the entry.

Place all of your belongings in a basket. Attempt to cover your privates with the tenugui.

Soap yourself up and hose yourself down before entering the bath. Enter slowly! The water is amazingly hot.

おんな Onna woman

おとこ Otoko man

Caution: make sure you choose the right bath. Women's curtain is usually pink or red. Men's curtain is blue.

If there is a rotemburo (outside bath) take another long soak and admire the view.

Dry yourself off back in the changing room.

Return to your room in your yukata and haori. Now you are dressed for dinner.

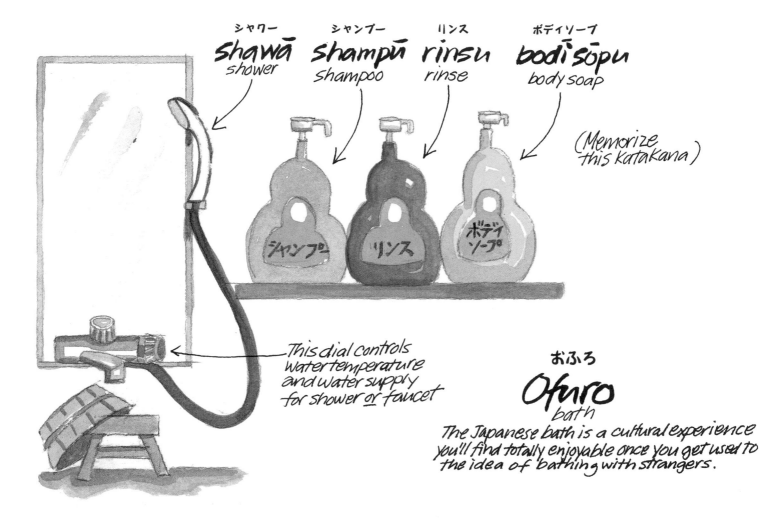

シャワー
shawā
shower

シャンプー
shampū
shampoo

リンス
rinsu
rinse

ボディソープ
bodi sōpu
body soap

(Memorize this katakana)

This dial controls water temperature and water supply for shower _or_ faucet

おふろ
Ofuro
bath

The Japanese bath is a cultural experience you'll find totally enjoyable once you get used to the idea of bathing with strangers.

かいせきりょうり
Kaiseki-ryōri
consists of several courses
of artistically arranged,
delicious seasonal foods but...

(some of it may be
unrecognizable to you.)
Often your meals are
served in your room.

てんぷら
tempura
deep-fried
battered prawns
and veggies

てんつゆ
tentsuyu
tempura
dipping
sauce

さしみ
Sashimi
raw fish
and prawn

ごまどうふ
goma dōfu
sesame tofu

にもの
nimono
boiled vegetables and
meat

すいもの
suimono
clear soup

うめしゅ
ume shu
plum
wine

vegetable
hors d'oeuvres
zensai
ぜんさい

ばんごはん
Ban gohan
dinner
(All this food is a serving for one person)

54

After dinner drag your overly full self to the Karaoke bar to entertain the other guests.

さけ
saké
rice wine and other forms of alcohol cost extra

メロン
meron
melon

さかなのてりやき
sakana-no-teriyaki
fish broiled with soy sauce, saké, mirin and sugar

なべもの
nabemono
meat, fish and vegetables cooked at the table

みそしる
miso shiru
miso soup

ちゃわんむし
chawan mushi
custard made from eggs and fish broth with delicious things inside.

つけもの
tsukemono
pickled veggies

にほんちゃ
nihon-cha
Japanese tea

こはん
gohan
cooked rice

The Grand Finale – rice, miso soup, tea and pickles

55

futon ふとん
Japanese bedding will be waiting for you when you return.

Have a good night's sleep and wake up hungry for a hearty breakfast.

うめぼし
ume boshi
pickled plum

ごはん
gohan cooked rice

おちゃ
Ocha green tea

なべ
nabe hot pot with meat and vegetables

サラダ
sarada salad

ひもの
himono dried fish

なっとう
natto sticky fermented soybeans

なまたまご
nama tamago raw egg

のり
nori dried seaweed

かまぼこ
kamaboko fish paste

つけもの
tsukemono pickled veggies

あさごはん
Asa gohan breakfast

miso shiru みそしる
miso soup

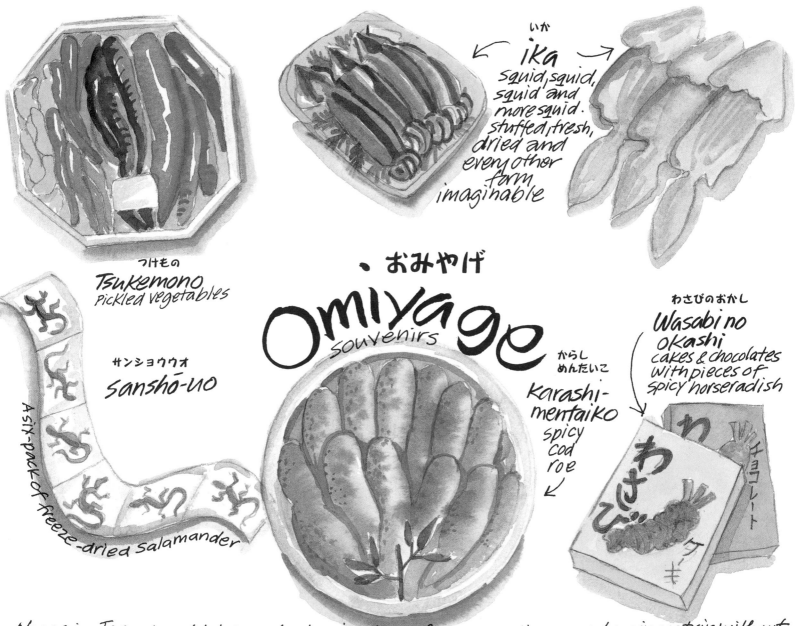

いか
ika
squid, squid, squid and more squid. stuffed, fresh, dried and every other form imaginable

つけもの
Tsukemono
Pickled vegetables

サンショウウオ
Sanshō-uo

A six-pack of freeze-dried salamander

・おみやげ
Omiyage
souvenirs

からし めんたいこ
Karashi-mentaiko
spicy cod roe

わさびのおかし
Wasabi no okashi
cakes & chocolates with pieces of spicy horseradish

No one in Japan would dream of returning home from a vacation or a business trip without buying a souvenir of food to show the folks back home what they missed. Coming from a culture where a typical gift would be a box of fudge or salt-water taffy - Japanese take-home took some getting used to. After sampling many - I must admit they are tasty.

Hey! Where do I put my legs?

Masu-zeki ますぜき
Traditional box seats that you share with three other people. Hopefully they will be tiny people.

A huge meal plus souvenirs can be purchased at an Ochaya (tea house) but you must share your 2 ft. of space with your food.

Zabuton ざぶとん

130 cm (4 ft deep)

130 cm (4'3" wide)

Osembei おせんべい
rice crackers

Obentō おべんとう
Japanese & Western lunch boxes

biru ビール
beer

Koka Kōra コカコーラ
Coca Cola

All this is a meal for one.

Kuri くり
chestnuts

Yakitori やきとり
chicken on a stick

Wagashi わがし
Japanese cakes

Soramame そらまめ
broad beans

mitsumame みつまめ
gelatin, sweet beans and fruit

Mikkusu sando itchi ミックスサンドイッチ
mixed sandwiches

Whole lot of eating going on!

Sumo Supper

Going to the sumo arena is a thrilling cultural experience - not only because of the sport. It is one big picnic for most of the spectators.

59

かいせきべんとう
Kaiseki bentō
An assortment of cooked and raw treats

パーティーセット
Pāti setto
An assortment of party foods

What's the big party? Why wasn't I invited?

7:00 am
Someone from the office is sent to stake out the picnic spot.

10:00 am
Mothers and children take their places.

11:00 am
Office workers begin

おにぎり

Onigiri
rice balls wrapped in nori

うなじゅうべんとう

Unajū bentō
grilled eel on rice

やきにく

Yaki niku
grilled beef

はなみ

Hanami
Cherry blossom-viewing party

The beautiful cherry blossom season in early April is a magical time. In Tokyo it becomes one big, week-long excuse to party. Eating portable foods and drinking saké while viewing the blossoms has been a tradition since ancient times.

Look longingly at a party in progress and you'll probably be invited to join in. If not—you can always start your own.

Kampai!
Cheers!
カンパイ！

to arrive.

7:00 pm
Serious partying begins

10:00 pm
Many parties are at a feverish pitch.

Ayu
grilled Japanese river trout

やたい ← **Yatai**
street stalls

まつり

Matsuri
Festival

Traditional festivals called Matsuri are connected to the agricultural calendar. No festival would be complete without the sights and smells of the many colorful food stalls lining the streets.

Yatai snacks are eaten while standing on the pavement-one of the few times it is acceptable to do so in Japan.

はちまき
← **Hachimaki**
head wrap

はんてん
Hanten →
short coat

じかたび
Jika tabi
split toed shoe socks →

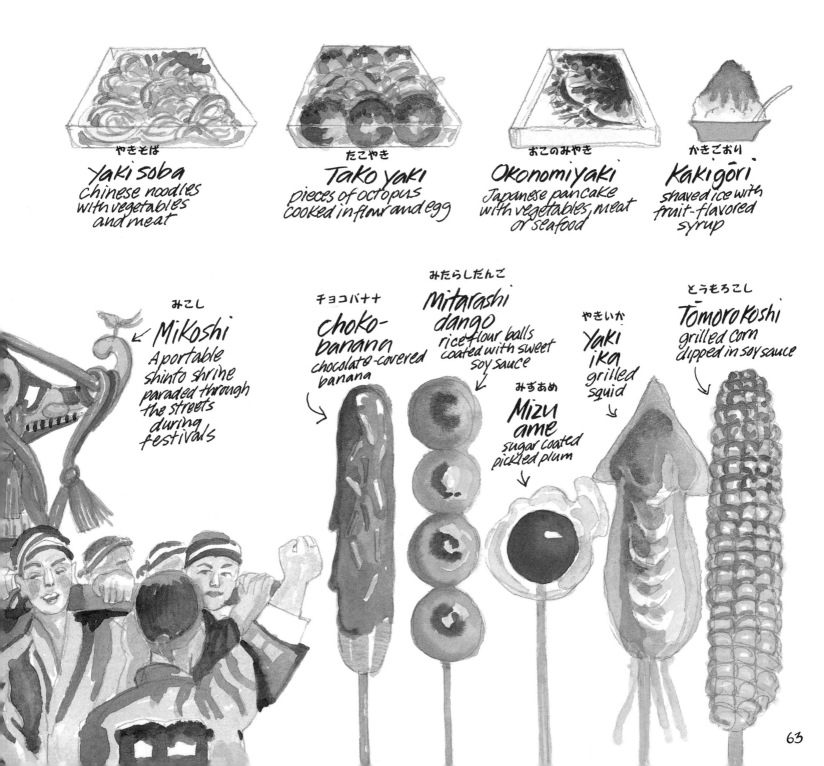

やきそば
Yaki soba
Chinese noodles with vegetables and meat

たこやき
Tako yaki
pieces of octopus cooked in flour and egg

おこのみやき
Okonomiyaki
Japanese pancake with vegetables, meat or seafood

かきごおり
Kakigōri
shaved ice with fruit-flavored syrup

みこし
← Mikoshi
A portable shinto shrine paraded through the streets during festivals

チョコバナナ
choko-banana
chocolate-covered banana

みたらしだんご
Mitarashi dango
rice flour balls coated with sweet soy sauce

みずあめ
Mizu ame
sugar coated pickled plum

やきいか
Yaki ika
grilled squid

とうもろこし
Tomorokoshi
grilled corn dipped in soy sauce

63

はつもうで
Hatsumōde
The first visit to a temple or shrine is a time to pray for prosperity in the coming year.

しめなわ
Shimenawa
Sacred ropes of rice-straw are hung at Shinto shrines to separate the pure world from the impure.

おしょうがつ
Oshōgatsu
Japanese New Year

The first three days of January have the invigorating feeling of festival. Many businesses, restaurants, food stores and museums are closed so it is a great time to people-watch at Buddhist temples and Shinto shrines.

はまや
Hamaya
Demon-quelling arrows

もちつき
Mochi-tsuki

You will see people pounding rice to make mochi.

あまざけ
Amazaké
Sweet sake is sold at yatai

じゅうばこ
Jūbako
Osechi-ryōri is served in a tiered lacquer box called a jūbako

おとそ
Otoso
Sake, with seven special herbs is served to every member of the household.

Nishimé にしめ
creatively-carved boiled vegetables

かまぼこ
Kamaboko
Boiled fish-paste cakes

Osechi-ryōri おせちりょうり
Beautifully-prepared, home-cooked food is eaten on the first three days of the New Year. The ingredients represent harvests from the fields, the sea and the mountains.

かずのこ
Kazunoko
Herring roe is a symbol of procreativity

えび Ebi
prawns symbolize long life.

Tazukuri たづくり
small fish symbolize a good harvest

くろまめ
Kuromamé
Black beans represent good health

としこしそば
Toshikoshi soba
symbolizing long life is enjoyed by families on New Year's eve before they set out to visit a temple or shrine.

おぞうに
Ozōni
A special soup containing mochi is eaten on New Year's Day

chew the mochi carefully - so that you don't choke—

and end up as a New Year fatality.

はる
Haru
Spring

なつ
Natsu
summer

あき
Aki
Fall

ふゆ
Fuyu
Winter

みづようかん
Mizu-yōkan, a type of jelly eaten chilled in summer ↓

わがし
Wagashi
Japanese Cakes

Kuri くり
chestnut

むしようかん
Mushi-yōkan is a mixture of An and wheat flour which is steamed in a mold.

とびん
Dobin
earthen teapot

Traditional Japanese cakes are very different from Western ones. Namagashi (uncooked cakes) are made from wheat flour, rice and a paste of sugar and beans, sweet potatoes, or chestnuts called An.

Namagashi are beautifully designed to match the seasons of the year. They must be eaten soon after purchasing.

66 Wagashi can be bought in department stores and speciality stores called Wagashi ya.

さくらもち
Sakura-mochi

Rice dumplings wrapped in cherry blossom leaves are eaten on Doll's Festival Day (Hina Matsuri) March 3rd

かしわもち
Kashiwa-mochi
Rice dumplings and sweet beans wrapped in oak leaves

Both are eaten on Children's Day (Kodomo no hi) May 5th →

ちまき
Chimaki
Rice dumplings wrapped in bamboo leaves.

おはぎ
Ohagi
→ Mochi wrapped in sweet bean paste is served during Spring and Fall Equinox

だいふく
Daifuku
A thin layer of mochi is wrapped around sweet bean paste

Monaka
もなか
A double wafer filled with sweet bean paste

くしだんご
Kushi dango
Rice balls on bamboo sticks either coated with An or soy sauce.

たいやき
Tai-yaki
pancakes filled with An and baked in molds

Imagawa-yaki
いまがわやき

ていしゅ
Teishu
→ Tea Master

ひがし
Higashi - Dry sweets eaten before drinking matcha

まっちゃ
Matcha
powdered green tea served during the tea ceremony

てやきせんべいや

手焼せんべい

Teyaki sembei ya *Rice cracker shop*

Try one piping hot and freshly dipped in soy in Asakusa or Kamakura.

↑

Teyaki sembei
てやきせんべい

ビール
Biru
Beer

← My favorite food group

かきピー
Kaki-pī
Crescent-shaped rice crackers with peanuts

おせんべい
The noisy snack

Osembei
Japanese rice crackers

えびづくし
Ebi Zukushi
Prawn crackers

ざらめせんべい
Zarame sembei
sweet rice crackers also have a slightly salty taste

There are basically two types of Japanese rice crackers— savory and sweet.
Savory sembei are made by steaming rice flour. Then they are baked and brushed with soy sauce. Sweet sembei are made from wheat flour, sugar and glucose.

Sembei come in all sizes and shapes and can fill a whole aisle in a supermarket.

They are delicious with green tea or cold beer.

Note: sembei can have a distinctive odor you may find unpleasant when you are not the one eating them.

What is that weird smell?

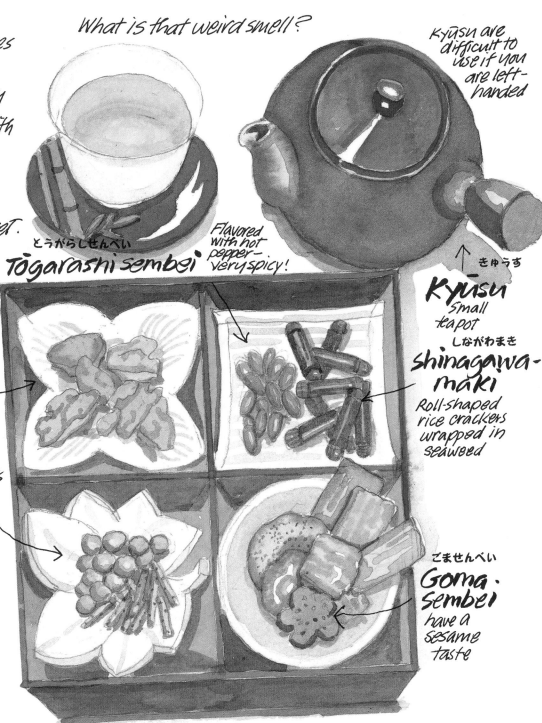

とうがらしせんべい
Tōgarashi sembei

Flavored with hot pepper— very spicy!

きゅうす
Kyusu
small teapot

Kyusu are difficult to use if you are left-handed

しながわまき
Shinagawa- maki
Roll-shaped rice crackers wrapped in seaweed

あげせんべい
Age sembei
Fried rice crackers

あられ **Arare**
small rice crackers

ごませんべい
Goma- sembei
have a sesame taste

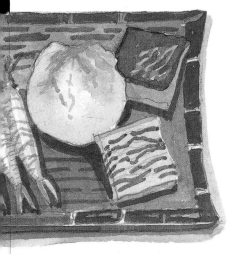

ごちそうさまでした
"Go chisō sama deshita"
"Thank you very much for the delicious food/drink"

After a meal it is polite to bow and say "go chisō sama deshita" to your host or chef.

It is considerate to finish all of your rice

Bones and other inedibles should be left on the side of your plate.

Replace the lid on your soupbowl.

Place your chopsticks back on the chopstick rest or in a knotted paper case to show you have finished eating.

Acknowledgment

I would like to thank the following friends who were kind enough to help me with my research and patient enough to let me sketch before they began eating.

To Elizabeth Andoh, Lyn Hall, Chikako Hisa, Junko Kimura, Sachiko Konami, Yuri Konomi, Miki and Kazu Ohyama, Yasuhiro Omura, Noriko Shiba, Mami Shimada, Junko Shimoyama, Kiyoko Sudou and Makiko and Masaaki Takagi:

Dōmo arigatō gozaimashita

Thank you very much!

Mata ne!

see you again

Published by Tuttle Publishing, an imprint of Periplus Editions (HK) Ltd

www.tuttlepublishing.com

ISBN 978-4-8053-1532-3
(Revised edition of previously published Squeamish About Sushi ISBN: 978-0-8048-3835-1, LCC Card No. 00019907)

Distributed by

North Ameri... Latin America & Europe
T...e ublishing
564 Innovation Drive
North Clarendon, VT 05759-9436 U.S.A.
Tel: 1 (802) 773-8930
Fam 1 (802) 773-6993
info@tuttlepublishing.com
www.tuttlepublishing.com

Japan
Tuttle Publishing
Yaekari Building 3rd Floor
5-4-12 Osaki
Shinagawa-ku
Tokyo 141-0032
Tel: (81) 3 5437-0171
Fax: (81) 3 5437-0755
sales@tuttle.co.jp
www.tuttle.co.jp

Asia Pacific
Berkeley Books Pte. Ltd.
3 Kallang Sector #04-01
Singapore 349278
Tel: (65) 67412178
Fam (65) 67412179
inquiries@periplus.com.sg
www.tuttlepublishing.com

25 24 23 22 21
10 9 8 7 6 5 4 3 2

Printed in Malaysia
2103TO

TUTTLE PUBLISHING® is a registered trademark of Tuttle Publishing, a division of Periplus Editions (HK) Ltd.

"Books to Span the East and West"

Tuttle Publishing was founded in 1832 in the small New England town of Rutland, Vermont [USA]. Our core values remain as strong today as they were then—to publish best-in-class books which bring people together one page at a time. In 1948, we established a publishing office in Japan—and Tuttle is now a leader in publishing English-language books about the arts, languages and cultures of Asia. The world has become a much smaller place today and Asia's economic and cultural influence has grown. Yet the need for meaningful dialogue and information about this diverse region has never been greater. Over the past seven decades, Tuttle has published thousands of books on subjects ranging from martial arts and paper crafts to language learning and literature—and our talented authors, illustrators, designers and photographers have won many prestigious awards. We welcome you to explore the wealth of information available on Asia at www.tuttlepublishing.com.

Nani ryōri desu ka? What type of cuisine do you serve? *Eigo no menyū wa arimasu ka?*

Naifu to fōku onegaishimasu. Knife and fork please. *Kore wa nan desu ka?* What is this? *Kore*

Mō hitotsu kudasai. Another please. *Oikura desu ka?* How much is it? *Oishi katta.* That was